Published in 2023 by Orange Mosquito
An Imprint of Welbeck Children's Limited
part of Welbeck Publishing Group.
Based in London and Sydney.
www.welbeckpublishing.com

In collaboration with Mosquito Books Barcelona S.L.

© Mosquito Books Barcelona, SL 2022
Text © Francesca Ferretti de Blonay 2022
Illustration © Carmen Casado 2022
Translation: Laura McGloughlin
Publisher: Margaux Durigon
Production: Jess Brisley

ISBN: 9781914519833
eISBN: 9781914519840

Printed in China
10 9 8 7 6 5 4 3 2 1

Francesca Ferretti de Blonay · Tània García

FRIDA DIEGO KAHLO & RIVERA

ORANGE
M·O·S·Q·U·I·T·O

MEXICO

The country was just emerging from a dictatorship. In a true economic boom, art and culture contributed enormously to drive the building of a new Mexico.

WHERE?

Mexico was swept up in its new intoxicating freedoms. The cities were swarming with people. Nights were lively and colorful. Social inequalities hadn't disappeared, but many people started living better, freer lives, and indulged in pleasures denied under the old dictatorship.

MEXICAN ART

Art celebrated the values and colors of Mexico and took inspiration from the history of the Mexican people, represented in the works of Diego Rivera and Frida Kahlo.

MURALISM

The painting of murals was an ancient art in Mexico. The scope of its public accessibility, on the streets of towns and cities, made it an ideal instrument for propaganda. Orozco, Siqueiros, and Rivera were the three great Mexican muralists of the time.

ABSTRACT ART

In the same era, numerous artists chose abstract art as a means of expression, signaling a break from realist or figurative art.

WHEN?

In 1928, the great artist Diego Rivera and the brilliant Frida Kahlo met. Although there were more than 20 years between them, their relationship was love at first sight.

1930s
BETWEEN TWO WARS

Crash of 1929: the New York Stock Exchange collapsed, banks went bankrupt, and people lost their jobs. It was a huge crisis!

1937: **Picasso** painted *Guernica*, condemning the horrors of the war and oppression in Spain.

The rise of extremism, with Hitler in Germany, Stalin in the USSR, Franco in Spain, and Mussolini in Italy, resulted in **World War II.**

Al Capone captured headlines in the United States. He became the most famous gangster of the twentieth century.

Paris dominated the world of fashion and **Coco Chanel** took part in her first fashion shows.

There were feminist protests, calling for women's right to vote. In France, feminist activist, existentialist philosopher, and writer **Simone de Beauvoir** became a feminist icon.

VOTES FOR WOMEN

German actress and singer **Marlene Dietrich** was recognized as the ninth greatest movie star of all time.

American singer and dancer **Josephine Baker** carried out an important role in the French resistance. She also made the Charleston dance fashionable in France.

The movie industry was flourishing, with great classics such as *King Kong*, *The Adventures of Robin Hood* and *Gone with the Wind*.

FRIDA

Frida Kahlo was born on July 6th, 1907, in
Coyoacán, Mexico. She suffered with childhood
polio, but in spite of the physical leg and foot
problems the disease gave her, Frida was a happy
child. At 15 she joined "Las Cachuchas" (The Caps),
a group of rebellious, intelligent, cultured students
who were always playing tricks in class.

THE ACCIDENT

At the age of 18, Frida was full of life and the world was her oyster!
Little did she imagine how much her life would change that September
day in 1925, when the bus she was traveling on crashed into a tram.
Many people died in the accident. Frida survived, but suffered multiple
fractures to her spinal column, right leg, ribs, clavicle, and pelvis.

A PAINTER IS BORN

Once she returned home from the hospital,
Frida had to stay still in bed, unable to move
for months. Frida's mother decided to install a
mirror and an easel over the bed, and to escape
her injured body, Frida began to paint.

Three months after the accident Frida was still bedridden and unable to move. Her boyfriend had left her, and the doctors didn't hold out much hope that she might be able to return to a normal life. Although her family rallied around her, it wasn't exactly fun. Within the four walls of her bedroom, with her face as the only model, Frida painted a series of self-portraits and they were very good! It felt good to be able to reflect the state of her mind through her paintings.

One day, against all odds, Frida walked again. It was an amazing moment! Although she couldn't escape metallic corsets and was still in a lot of pain, Frida's desire to live spurred her on. She was brimming with energy, just like her beloved country Mexico, and she felt like she had been reborn and given another chance.

As Frida's rehabilitation progressed and she was able to walk more easily, she immersed herself in the harmonious chaos and new freedoms of Mexico in search of inspiration. For Frida, suffering and the yearning to live were two constants in her life.

ARTISTIC UNIVERSE:
her own reality, Mexico

Frida Kahlo focused on self-portraits. Of the almost 200 works she painted throughout her life, 55 were self-portraits. It was as though, after the accident, she'd given herself a new identity.

She created a colorful aesthetic universe full of energy, like the Mexico that inspired her: its vegetation, its colors, its pre-Columbian art, the traditional dresses that she usually wore, as well as the country's indigenous roots and the symbols she found in them.

Frida didn't really have any formal art training; she was a free spirit. However, traces of the Renaissance art style or early Matisse can be seen in her work. Frida was, above all, a cultured, passionate, and avant-garde woman who painted her reality, her suffering, her condition as a woman, and her Communist opinions with great realism; some would say even magic realism.

AMOR

THE PERSONALITY

Frida was a passionate woman. Her ideas, her friends, and her art were all part of the same thing to her. Her paintings reflected her passion. Her humor, along with her exotic beauty, made Frida attractive and fascinating. Although she didn't sell many paintings during her life, Frida's work had an enormous impact in the art world.

THEMES

Frida's accident shaped her destiny and her work. From that point on, Frida Kahlo set about expressing her pain. Without reservation, she painted her reality, her experience as a woman, and later as a wife. She laid bare her private life. She also talked about her duality, sometimes presenting herself as a woman and at other times as a man. It wasn't long before Frida was considered a symbol of femininity, and not only in Mexico, but all over the world. Frida became pregnant three times, but sadly, none of her pregnancies came to term. Frida described this deep sorrow on numerous canvases. She transformed her suffering into art.

And finally, we mustn't forget Diego, her husband, who became the central theme of her work and was there for it all. He was everywhere: in her painting, in her spirit, and in her heart. In fact, Frida wrote these words in her private diary:

Diego — my **husband**

Diego — my **friend**

Diego — my **mother**

Diego — my **father**

Diego — my **child**

Diego — **me**

Diego — **universe**

DIEGO

Diego Rivera was born on December 8th, 1886, in Guanajuato, a mining city in central Mexico. He was a curious boy who spent all his time drawing. After finishing his studies in Fine Arts, he left home to explore his country. Later he obtained a grant to study in Europe. He was looking forward to it! In Paris he met Picasso, Braque, and many other artists before returning to Mexico.

MURALIST

Rivera also painted on an easel, but he was better known around the world for his murals. Rivera was famous for his work and was admired by many people, especially as he played a huge part in the renewal of Mexican culture, telling the stories of the origins of Mexico and its people in his large frescoes.

COMMUNIST

Considered by some as a genius and by others as an ogre or a hustler, Diego was above all an idealist who wanted to change society. With these ideals he would conquer the world. His art and his commitment to change were the only things that mattered to him. Along with Frida, of course!

BACKGROUND

On his return from Europe, Diego Rivera created his first mural. Up on his scaffold, in his blue overalls, he could spend 12 hours straight painting. His wife, Lupe Marín, would bring him lunch and leave again, often angry after having argued with him. Their marital fights made headlines.

UNIVERSE

Like the painters of the Italian Renaissance, Diego liked to make an impact. He used art to educate. He wanted to communicate the values of Mexico to the people so that they could identify with them. His large frescoes told much more than a single story and the ideas and themes in them were easy to understand. Rivera was a humanist; he believed that human welfare and interests and values were the most important things in life. If people lived by these ideals and took responsibility for their own lives, then humanity collectively could build a better society. This belief was reflected in his art where the human being was the central element.

RECOGNITION

Diego was an extravagant person, and his larger–than–life personality made him famous. Recognized throughout the world, his work earned him international renown and the respect of artists of his time.

THEMES

Diego would walk around with a notebook and write down everything he saw. He painted the world that surrounded him, the world of his time: the rise of the rich, industrialization, accumulation of wealth, and the poor's demands for the fair distribution of resources. Rivera saw his art as a service for the people. He wanted to grant everyone their rightful place and honor all Mexicans through their origins. His passion for pre-Columbian art was a constant throughout his life.

He also created a collection of thousands of pieces of pre-Hispanic art at the Museo Anahuacalli. Apart from his large frescoes, he continued to paint indigenous scenes and self-portraits. He wasn't intimidated by any form of art. It was as though he had been born with a paintbrush in his hand and with his great talent, he made use of all the resources available to him.

FIRST CONTACT

Frida was a young woman when she met Diego Rivera. At that time, he was working on a mural in the amphitheater of Frida's school. Rivera was quite the celebrity and the young Frida spent hours watching him on his scaffold.

UNION

The official meeting of the two artists took place after a Communist Party meeting in 1928, at the house of the renowned photographer Tina Modotti. It was there that the most famous parties in Mexico took place. After having put the accident behind her, Frida only wanted one thing: to enjoy herself! From then on, Frida and Diego were never apart, or almost never...

ADMIRATION

One day Frida invited Diego to her studio.
The painter was surprised by the depth of her
portraits and asked her to show him more.
This was the moment that their story of love
and mutual admiration began.

THE ART

Diego painted Frida as a young revolutionary in one of his murals. Later, when Frida became his wife, he encouraged her to paint; he had become her greatest admirer. For her part, Frida played the dutiful role of the wife of an accomplished painter, and accompanied Diego to San Francisco, New York, and Detroit. Her personality and exotic beauty were almost as seductive as the talent of her husband.

THE LOVE

On August 21st, 1929, Frida Kahlo and Diego Rivera got married. They were like two sides of the same coin: they shared the same taste for art, political involvement, and love for Mexico. The 21-year age gap between them didn't matter.

Frida and Diego shared a passionate and extraordinary love and appreciated each other enormously. The unique house they built as their marital home, when they returned to Mexico from the USA, was a physical reflection of their incredible love for each other.

"Two houses facing each other, the big one pink and the small one blue, joined but separate, like a witty response to the impossible equation of the couple: to live together but not too much."

Claire Berest, *Rien n'est noir*

CONNECTION

Frida painted her inner world, while Diego observed the external world. Each had their own universe! Although Diego appeared in some of his wife's paintings, both artists kept their individual art styles, while still acknowledging the other's.

SEDUCTIVE AND EXPLOSIVE

Frida and Diego made a well-respected pair, and together they seduced their followers as much through their talent as by their personalities. Their relationship wasn't all smooth sailing. At times, their passion erupted in arguments and disagreements. But in spite of this, their love was ever present.

EMANCIPATION

In 1938, Frida exhibited her work in a gallery in Manhattan, New York for the first time. It was an immediate success. Shortly afterward she signed up for an exhibition in Paris organized by André Breton, the leader of surrealism. Her work was praised by the great painters and artists Picasso, Duchamp, Max Ernst, and Joan Miró.

RECONNECTING UNTIL THE END

By 1939, Frida and Diego's relationship had hit a low point and they decided to get divorced that same year. Frida moved back to her family home (known as the Blue House) and buried herself in her work and painted some of her most beautiful pictures. But she felt very alone and was drinking a lot, and her health deteriorated. She decided to fill the house with a menagerie of animals—fawns, monkeys, turtledoves, parrots, parakeets, and dogs...and gradually, with the help of her sister Cristina and her friends, Frida rediscovered her joy in living. She started seeing Diego again, and the couple remarried in 1941.

IN SICKNESS AND IN HEALTH

Frida's health went from bad to worse, so much so that she had to attend her final exhibition in 1953 in a bed placed in the center of the room. Pumped full of medication and in a lot of pain, Frida got through the event with Diego by her side.

Frida died on July 13th, 1954, in the Blue House. There, Diego built a magnificent museum and garden in her memory. On November 24th, 1957, Diego himself died, leaving behind important pieces of their joint work and the fascinating life story of their unique and dynamic relationship.

In her time, Frida was considered the wife of the great muralist Diego Rivera. Today, it is Diego who is known as the husband of the great Frida Kahlo. Frida's commitment to sharing the stories of the most disadvantaged people through her art inspires respect, and her captivating femininity continues to fascinate. And as for her famous eyebrows in the shape of wings, well these are renowned worldwide!

INSPIRATION

Frida and Diego lived in a time of artistic euphoria, shaken by two devastating world wars and various crises. It was as though the artists felt an urgency to express themselves and produce unforgettable works of art.

LEGENDARY

Frida is everywhere: on cups, T-shirts, oven gloves, phone covers ... there are countless products bearing her portraits in the vibrant colors of Mexico. Frida-mania in play! Her work is shown in the most iconic museums around the world. Like other geniuses, Frida has become an icon.

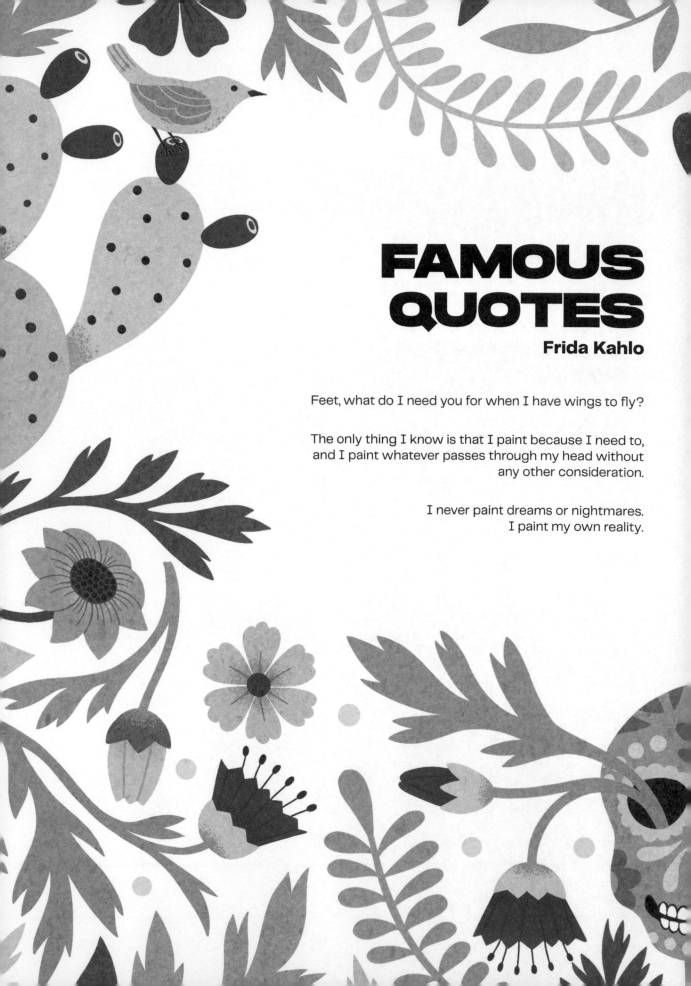

FAMOUS QUOTES

Frida Kahlo

Feet, what do I need you for when I have wings to fly?

The only thing I know is that I paint because I need to, and I paint whatever passes through my head without any other consideration.

I never paint dreams or nightmares. I paint my own reality.

I only want three things in life:
    1. Live with Diego.
    2. Continue painting.
    3. Belong to the Communist Party.

I want my work to contribute to the struggle for peace and freedom.

There is nothing more beautiful than laughter. Laughing is one of the great pleasures of life: it is shared and makes us see its beauty.

Can verbs be made up? I'll tell you one. I heaven you, so my wings will open wide to love you boundlessly.

FAMOUS QUOTES

Diego Rivera

July 13th, 1954, was the most tragic day of my life. I had lost my beloved
Frida forever. Too late now I realized that the most wonderful part
of my life had been my love for Frida.

[Frida is] acid and tender, hard as steel and delicate and
fine as a butterfly's wing.

Lovable as a beautiful smile, and as profound and
cruel as the bitterness of life.

My style was born like a child, in a moment,
with the difference that this birth took place at the end of a painful,
35-year gestation.

I painted as naturally as I breathed,
spoke or sweated.

I'm not a pessimist, rather a hedonist and an epicurean.

FRIDA AND DIEGO RIVERA

A WORK BY FRIDA KAHLO

In 1931, Frida and Diego were in San Francisco. Frida had suffered her second miscarriage. Her leg was hurting, and she had to take to her bed once again. During this time, she painted various canvases, including a magnificent portrait of herself and Diego. This painting represented their love. In it, Diego appeared with an artist's palette, large feet, and a considerably more imposing body than Frida, even bearing in mind their difference in stature: he measured 6 feet, 1 inch in height, and she was 5 feet, 3 inches tall.

Frida is shown with tiny feet, as if to highlight the respect she had for the great painter that Diego was. It's notable that the faces of both artists have a sad look, a sign that the couple was going through a difficult time.

Themes: love, Diego, a woman's position in relation to a man, the torment of love.

Technique: oil on canvas, 39.5 x 31 inches. The painting can be found in the San Francisco Museum of Modern Art.

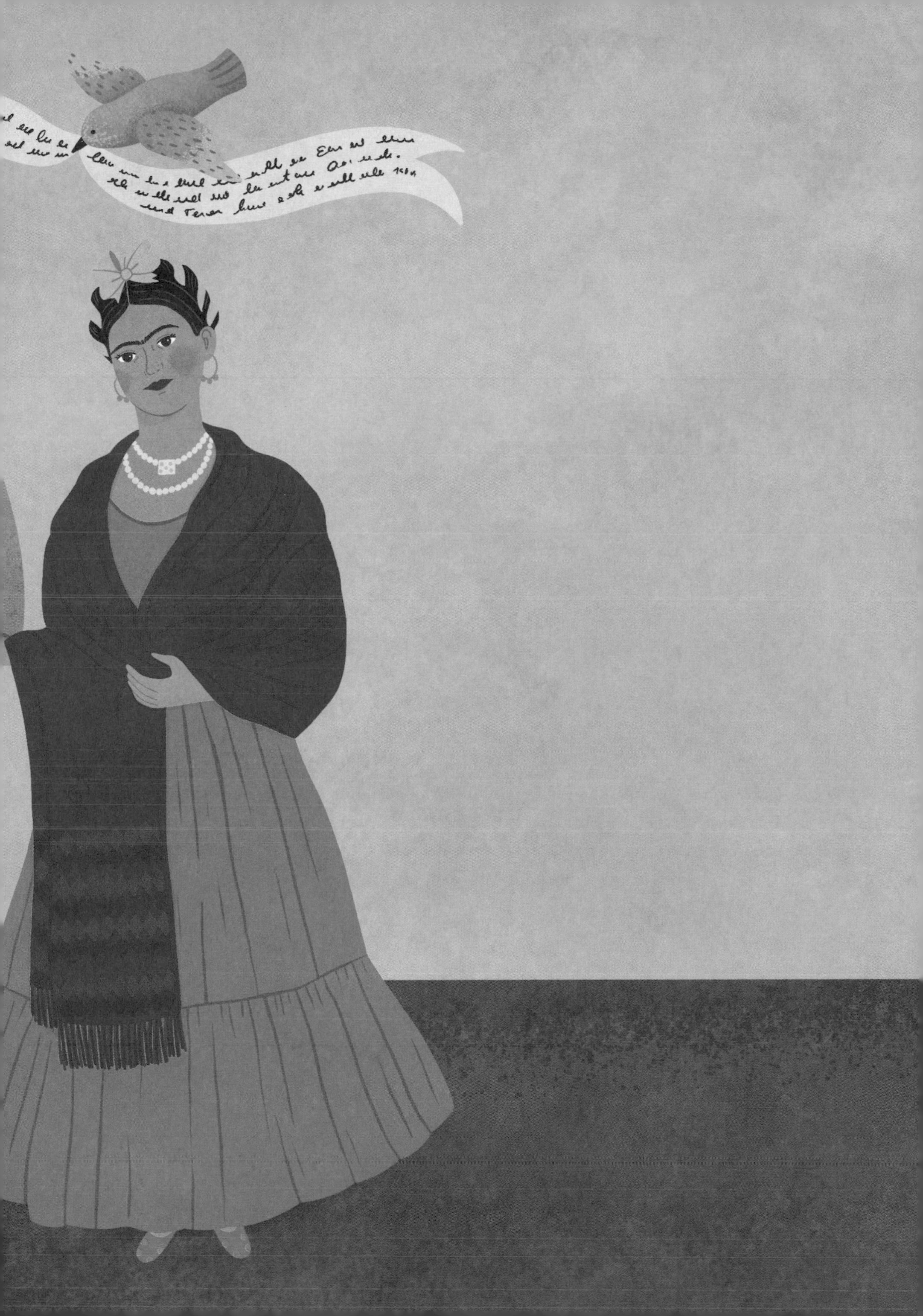

MAN, CONTROLLER OF THE UNIVERSE

A WORK BY DIEGO RIVERA

In 1933, by request of the multi-millionaire Nelson Rockefeller, Diego Rivera accepted a commission to create a huge mural for the shopping center that the grandson of the oil magnate was building.

The world was in the middle of an economic crisis and the theme, "Man at the Crossroads Looking with Hope and High Vision to the Choosing of a New and Better Future," that Nelson insisted on struck a chord with the idealistic painter.

Rivera got to work. After two months the fresco had taken shape. Some well-known faces stood out: Karl Marx and Vladimir Lenin, two major figures of Communism. The controversial piece caught the attention of the media. One malicious journalist wrote that it was a revolutionary work mocking its patron.

Themes: the future of man, the opposition between two models of society: the world of the rich (capitalism) and the world of the poor (communism).

Technique: fresco painting, based on architectural painting used in construction; grisaille (black and white technique that resembles bas-relief).

Nelson was hurt by the journalist's comment, and he asked Diego to remove the portraits of Lenin and Marx. Diego refused, and Nelson fired the painter. Diego flew into a rage, and although he had been paid well, he left the work unfinished.

Later Diego and Frida returned to their country, and while he was painting the same mural at Palacio de Bellas Artes (Palace of Fine Arts) in Mexico City he heard that his work in the Rockefeller Center had been destroyed. From an aesthetic point of view, this was not good, but it was powerfully symbolic.

ARTISTS AND FRIENDS

LUPE MARÍN

The Mexican writer was Diego Rivera's second wife, before Frida Kahlo. She had two children with the painter.

ALEJANDRO GÓMEZ ARIAS

Frida Kahlo's first love. Alejandro was with her on the day of the accident which turned her existence into agony. Their friendship lasted all their lives.

TINA MODOTTI

Famous photographer, artist, and revolutionary of Italian origin. She was an educated woman who never stopped condemning the injustices that surrounded her.

LEÓN TROTSKI

Russian revolutionary persecuted by Stalin. Trotsky and his wife sought asylum in Mexico and were made welcome in the Blue House by Diego and Frida. A passionate, but forbidden relationship developed between Leon and Frida.

ANDRÉ BRETON

French writer and poet. He was considered the father of the Surrealist movement in France. Thanks to him, Frida Kahlo had her first exhibition in France.

NICKOLAS MURAY

American photographer of Hungarian origin. Frida met him at her first exhibition of paintings in New York.

GLOSSARY

Abstract art: a form of art with no recognizable subject or image from our everyday lives. It is shapes, lines, colors, texture.

Communism/Communist Party: a government and economic system where people share the wealth they create. Individuals do not own properties and the goal is to make life fair and equal for everyone.

Dictatorship: a government where full power is held by a person or a small group. Their ruler is called a dictator.

Frescoes: a painting that is done on a wall.

Industrialization: a process using better technology to make things in an easier, faster and cheaper way.

Karl Marx: a German journalist, editor and socialist theorist. He wrote 'The Communist Manifesto' in 1848 and is popularly regarded as the father of modern socialism, or Marxism.

Vladimir Lenin: a Russian revolutionary and politician. He was the founder of the Soviet Union, the world's first communist country.

Muralist: a painter who creates a large picture on the wall of a room or building.

Nelson Rockefeller: an American businessman and politician. He was the 41st Vice President of the United States and previously governor of New York. His paternal grandfather was one of the wealthiest people in the United States after founding the Standard Oil Company.

Magnate: a very wealthy and powerful businessperson.

Propaganda: a form of communication to influence public opinion via facts, arguments, rumours, half-truths or lies.

Surrealism: an artistic movement born in France which placed great importance on unconscious thinking and dreams for overcoming reality.